This book is dedicated to Mary Cummiskey Miller and Janice Mann/ Carolyn Carey and to all of the grandmas who have brought pure joy and endless love into our lives. You are forever in our hearts.

I know the whole alphabet by heart.

I can count to 1 million.

I can button my shirt.

I can zip my coat. ☑

I can do a lot of 5 year old things.

I still want to do more things!

BFFs

I have a lot of friends and they can do a lot of things too.

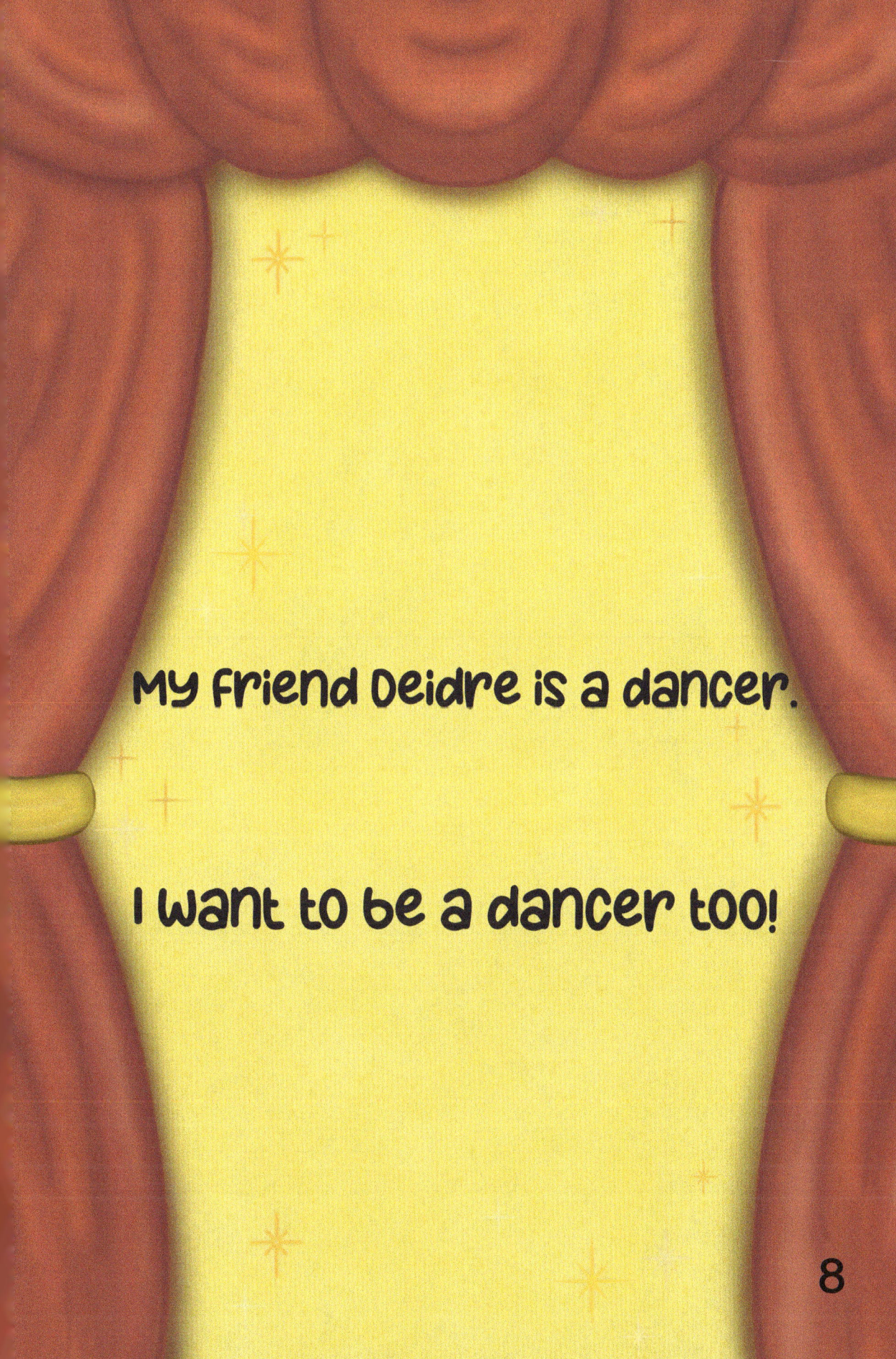

My friend Deidre is a dancer.

I want to be a dancer too!

I put on my tights.

I put on my ballet shoes.

I put on my ballerina dress.

My tights are too tight.
My shoes are too slippery.
My dress keeps falling down.

I am not Gracie dancer.

My friend Sonia is a singer.

I want to be a singer too!

I get my microphone. 🎵

I get my speaker. 🎵

I get on the stage. 🎵

My microphone sounds funny.
My speaker is too loud! I fell off the stage!

I am not Gracie Singer.

My friend Brenda is a builder.

I want to be a builder too!

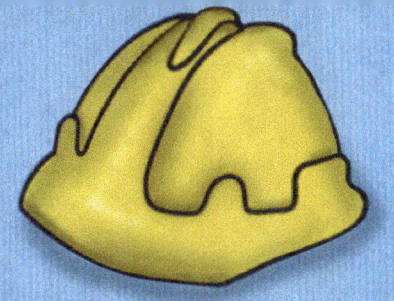

I get a hammer.
I get some nails.
I get a piece of wood.

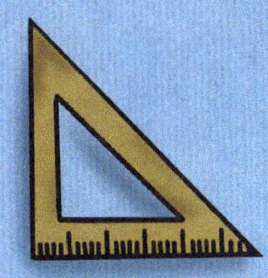

The hammer is too heavy. The nails won't stay still. Ouch! I hit my thumb with the hammer.

I am not Gracie builder.

I walked to my grandma's house. She lives down the street from me. I always go to my grandma's house when I am sad, or happy, or to play. I love my grandma.

"Hi there Gracie! Why do you look so sad?" my grandma asked.

"I tried to be good at things like all of my friends, but I didn't like any of the things that they like", I said.

"Well Gracie, maybe you just need to find your own thing to be good at", said my grandma.

But how do I find my own thing?

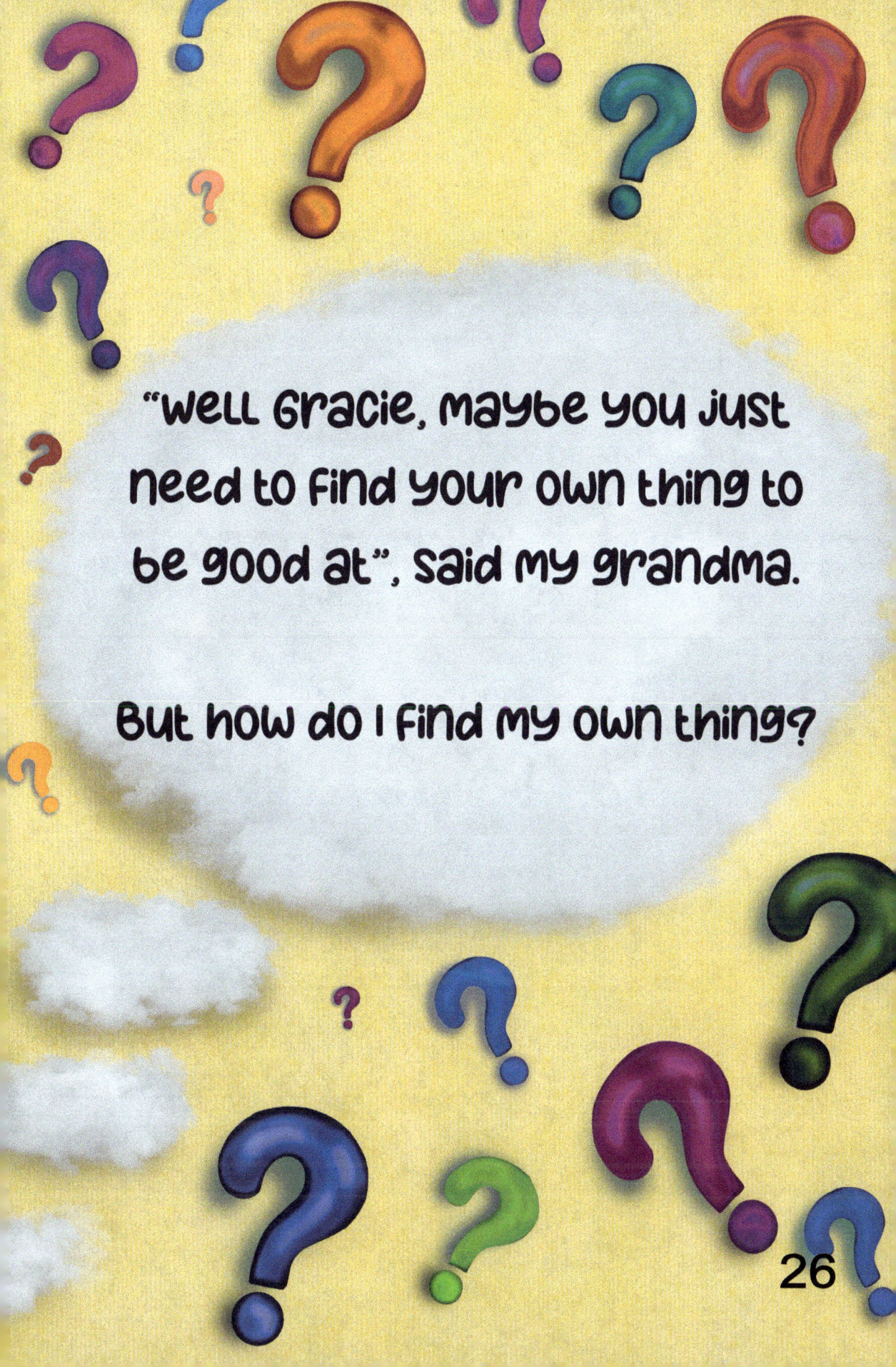

"Let's take a break for now", grandma said.

"Let's go water the flowers, that always cheers you up."

Grandma has very pretty flowers in her garden.

She has sunflowers and lilacs and marigolds.

She has a lot more but these are my favorite.

I put on my hat.

I put on my gloves.

I fill up my watering can.

I feel the breeze and it is gentle on my face.

I smell the lilacs and it makes me smile.

I love the way the watering can makes little raindrops on the flowers and leaves.

Grandma + Gracie

"It! My thing! I found my thing!", I said.

"Oh that's great sweetheart!", grandma said and she gave me a hug.

"Well, what's your thing?" grandma asked.

"Gardening!" I exclaimed.

I am Gracie Gardener.

www.ingramcontent.com/pod-product-compliance
Lightning Source LLC
LaVergne TN
LVHW081454060526
838201LV00050BA/1795